ERIC CLAPTON

CONTENTS

W9-CBC-106

Cover photo © Michael Putland/Retna UK

Tracking, mixing, and mastering by Jake Johnson
All guitars by Doug Boduch
Bass by Tom McGirr
Saxophone, Keyboards by Warren Wiegratz
Drums by Scott Schroedl

ISBN 0-634-08017-2

Visit Hal Leonard Online at www.halleonard.com

HAL•LEONARD®
CORPORATION
7777 W. BLUEMOUND RD. P.O. BOX 13819
MILWAUKEE, WISCONSIN 53213

Guitar Notation Legend

THE MUSICAL STAFF shows pitches and rhythms and is divided by bar lines into measures. Pitches are named after the first seven letters of the alphabet.

TABLATURE graphically represents the guitar fingerboard. Each horizontal line represents a string, and each number represents a fret.

4th string, 2nd fret   1st & 2nd strings open, played together   open D chord

HALF-STEP BEND: Strike the note and bend up 1/2 step.

WHOLE-STEP BEND: Strike the note and bend up one step.

GRACE NOTE BEND: Strike the note and bend up as indicated. The first note does not take up any time.

SLIGHT (MICROTONE) BEND: Strike the note and bend up 1/4 step.

BEND AND RELEASE: Strike the note and bend up as indicated, then release back to the original note. Only the first note is struck.

PRE-BEND: Bend the note as indicated, then strike it.

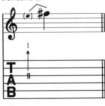

VIBRATO: The string is vibrated by rapidly bending and releasing the note with the fretting hand.

PALM MUTING: The note is partially muted by the pick hand lightly touching the string(s) just before the bridge.

HAMMER-ON: Strike the first (lower) note with one finger, then sound the higher note (on the same string) with another finger by fretting it without picking.

PULL-OFF: Place both fingers on the notes to be sounded. Strike the first note and without picking, pull the finger off to sound the second (lower) note.

LEGATO SLIDE: Strike the first note and then slide the same fret-hand finger up or down to the second note. The second note is not struck.

SHIFT SLIDE: Same as legato slide, except the second note is struck.

TRILL: Very rapidly alternate between the notes indicated by continuously hammering on and pulling off.

TAPPING: Hammer ("tap") the fret indicated with the pick-hand index or middle finger and pull off to the note fretted by the fret hand.

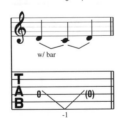

NATURAL HARMONIC: Strike the note while the fret-hand lightly touches the string directly over the fret indicated.

PINCH HARMONIC: The note is fretted normally and a harmonic is produced by adding the edge of the thumb or the tip of the index finger of the pick hand to the normal pick attack.

TREMOLO PICKING: The note is picked as rapidly and continuously as possible.

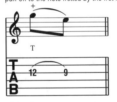

VIBRATO BAR DIVE AND RETURN: The pitch of the note or chord is dropped a specified number of steps (in rhythm) then returned to the original pitch.

VIBRATO BAR SCOOP: Depress the bar just before striking the note, then quickly release the bar.

VIBRATO BAR DIP: Strike the note and then immediately drop a specified number of steps, then release back to the original pitch.

Additional Musical Definitions

 (accent)   • Accentuate note (play it louder)

(staccato)   • Play the note short

D.S. al Coda   • Go back to the sign (𝄋), then play until the measure marked *"To Coda"*, then skip to the section labelled *"Coda."*

D.C. al Fine   • Go back to the beginning of the song and play until the measure marked *"Fine"* (end).

Fill   • Label used to identify a brief melodic figure which is to be inserted into the arrangement.

N.C.   • Instrument is silent (drops out).

• Repeat measures between signs.

1. ‖ 2.   • When a repeated section has different endings, play the first ending only the first time and the second ending only the second time.

Change the World

featured on the Motion Picture Soundtrack PHENOMENON

Words and Music by Wayne Kirkpatrick, Gordon Kennedy and Tommy Sims

Chorus

3rd time, substitute Fill 1

change _____ the world. ___ I will be __ the sun - light _ in your

u - ni - verse. __ You would think _ my love _ was real - ly

To Coda ⊕

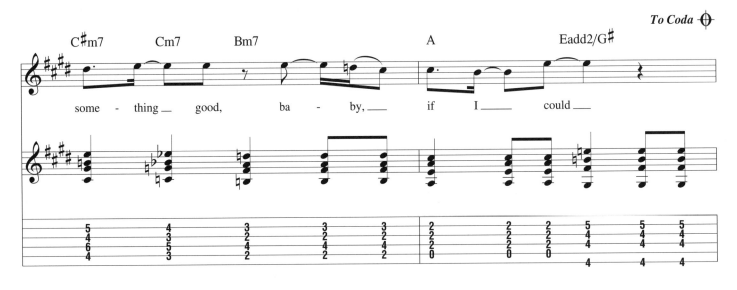

some - thing _ good, ba - by, __ if I ___ could ___

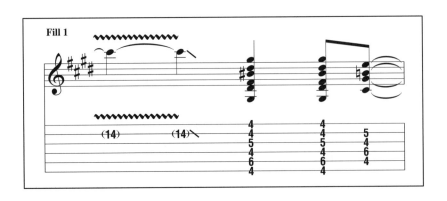

Fill 1

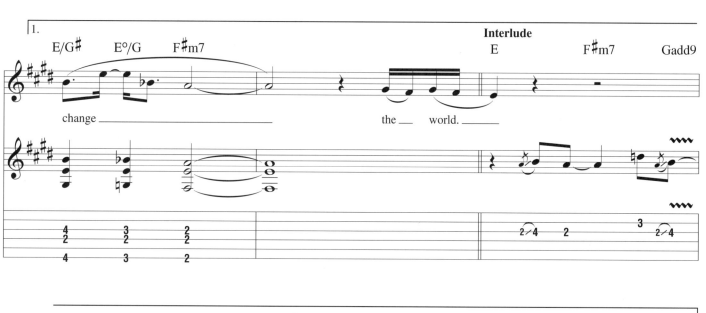

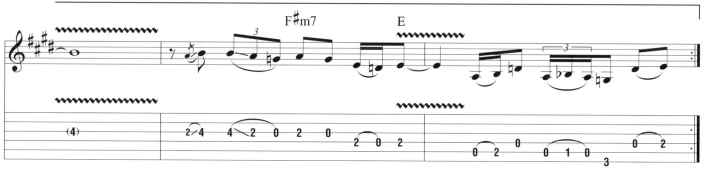

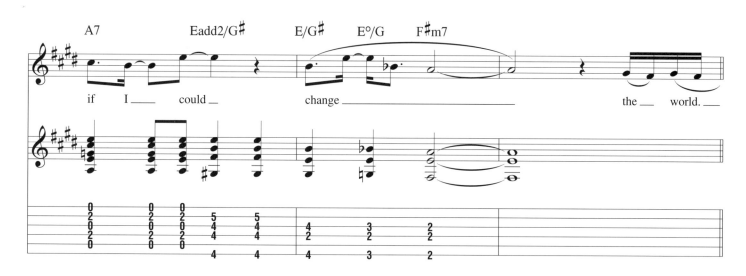

Guitar Solo

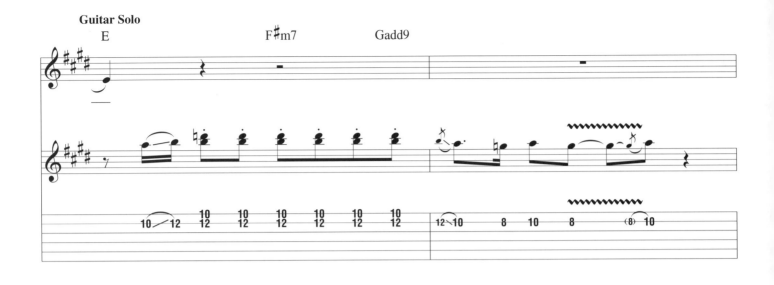

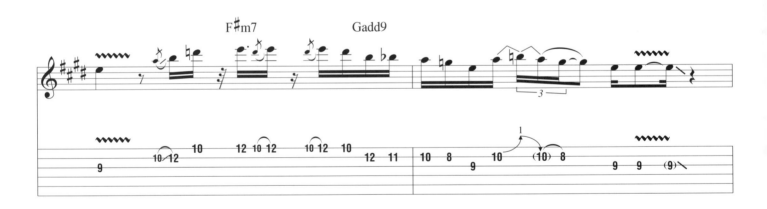

D.S. al Coda

8

Additional Lyrics

2. If I could be king,
   Even for a day,
   I'd take you as my queen,
   I'd have it no other way.
   And our love would rule
   In this kingdom we have made.
   Till then I'd be a fool,
   Wishing for the day.

Badge

Words and Music by Eric Clapton and George Harrison

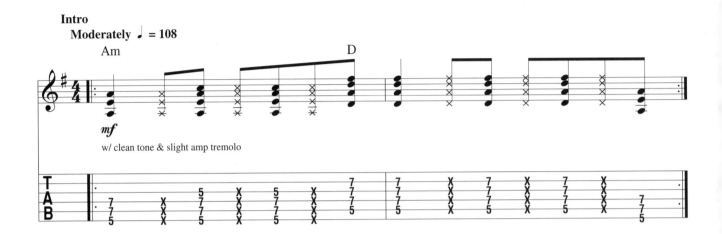

1. Think - in' 'bout the times you drove ____ in my car. ____
2. *See additional lyrics*

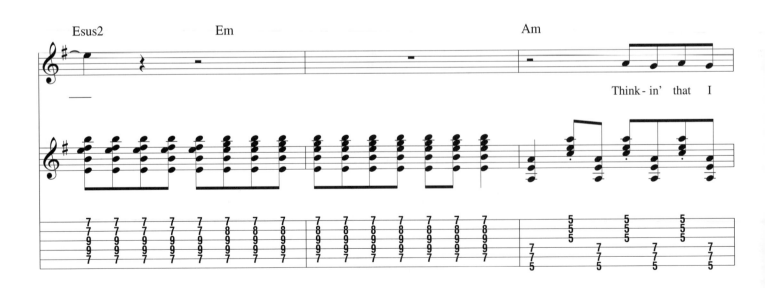

Think - in' that I

might have drove ___ you too far. ___

1.
And I'm think-in' 'bout the love that you made on my ta - ble.

2.
Then I told you 'bout our kid, now he's mar-ried to Ma -

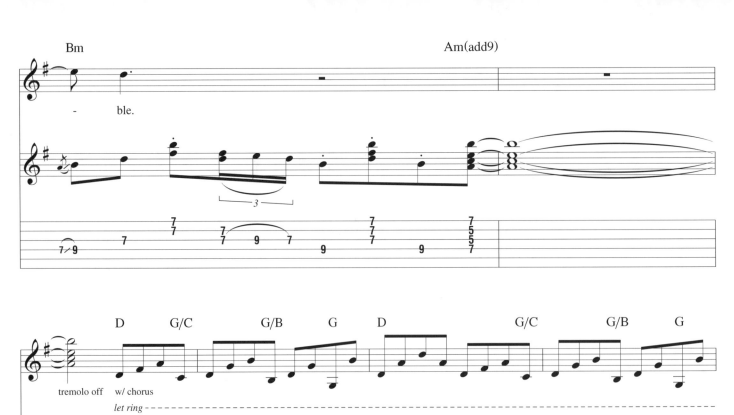

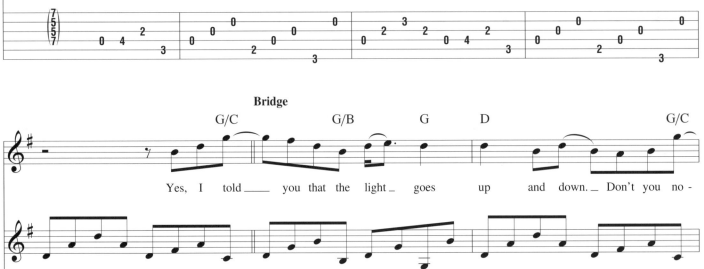

Bridge

Yes, I told _____ you that the light _ goes up and down. _ Don't you no-

- tice how the wheel _ goes 'round? And you bet - ter pick your-self up

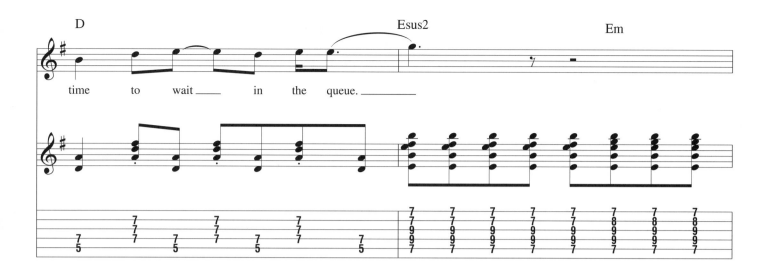

time to wait ___ in the queue. _____

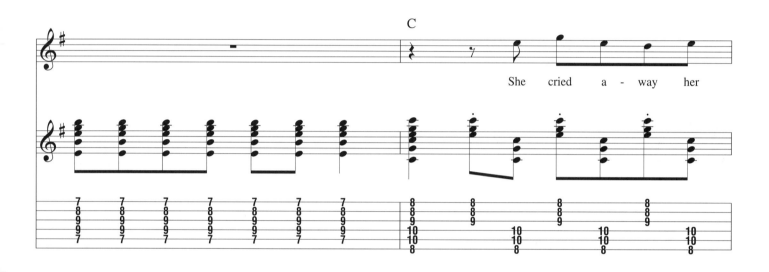

She cried a - way her

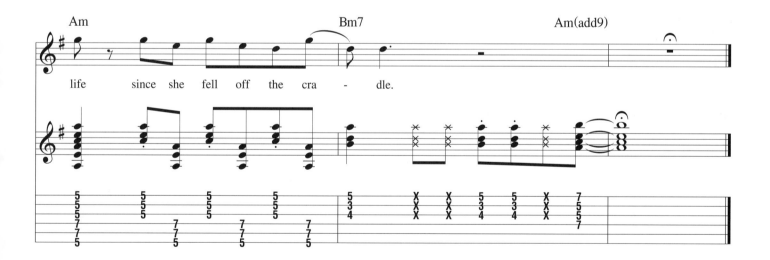

life since she fell off the cra - dle.

Additional Lyrics

2. I told you not to wander 'round in the dark.
   I told you 'bout the swans, that they live in the park.
   Then I told you 'bout our kid now he's married to Mable.

Bell Bottom Blues

Words and Music by Eric Clapton

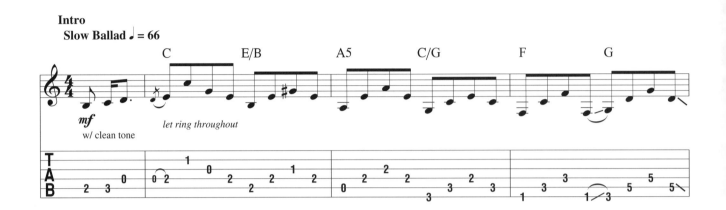

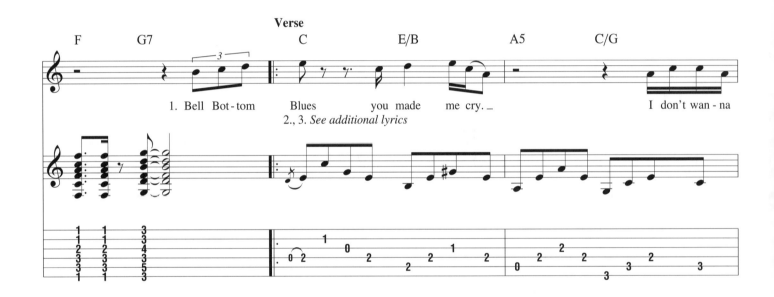

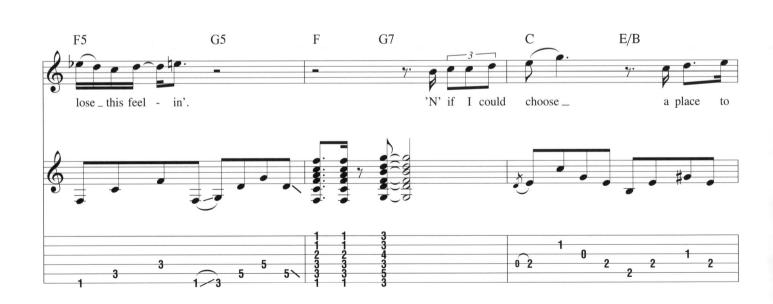

⊕ Coda

Outro-Chorus

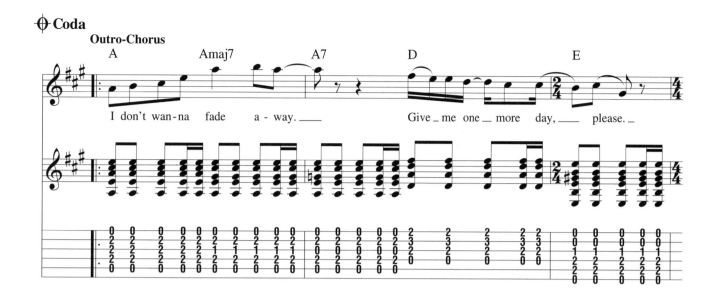

I don't wan-na fade a - way. ___ Give _ me one _ more day, ___ please. _

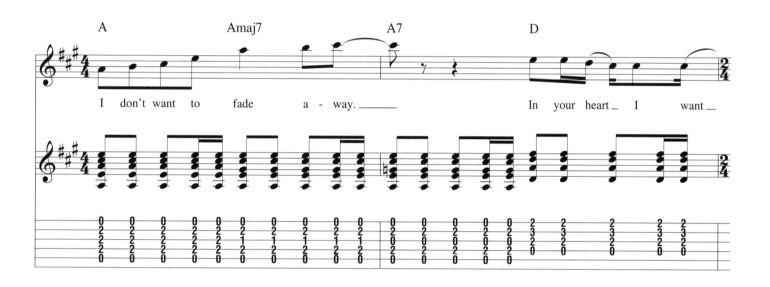

I don't want to fade a - way. _____ In your heart _ I want _

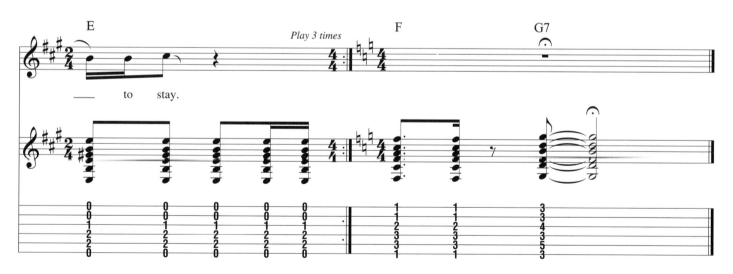

___ to stay.

Play 3 times

Additional Lyrics

2. It's all wrong, but it's alright.
   The way that you treat me baby, mm.
   Once I was strong, but I lost the fight;
   You won't find a better loser.

3. Bell Bottom Blues, don't say, "Goodbye."
   We're surely gonna meet again.
   And if we do, don't you be surprised
   If you find me with another lover. Oh.

Cocaine

Words and Music by J.J. Cale

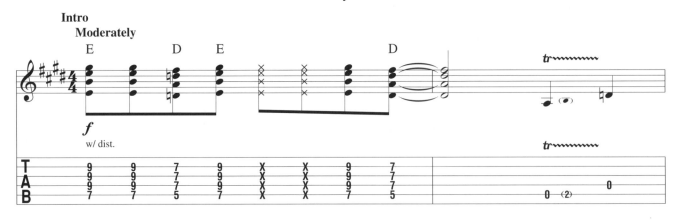

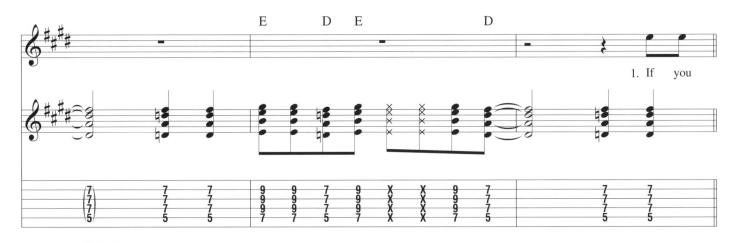

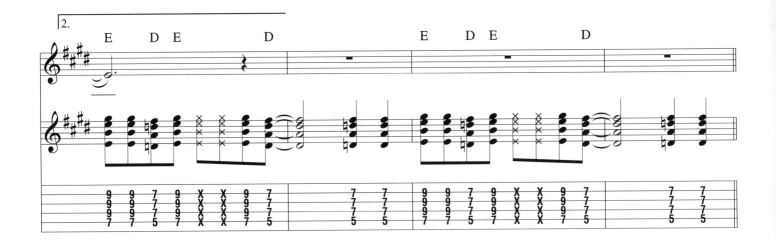

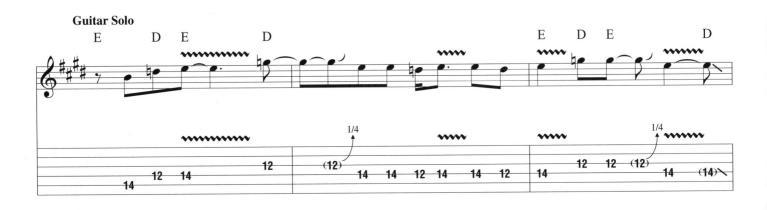

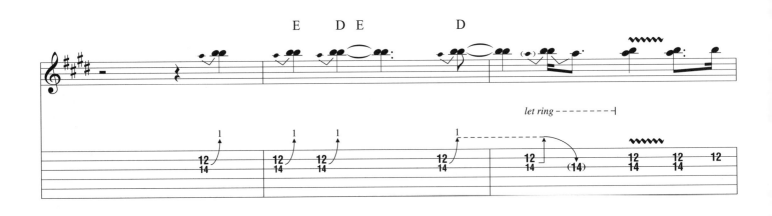

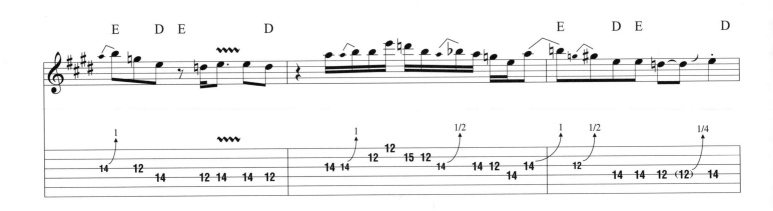

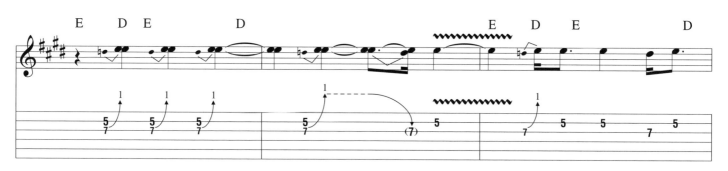

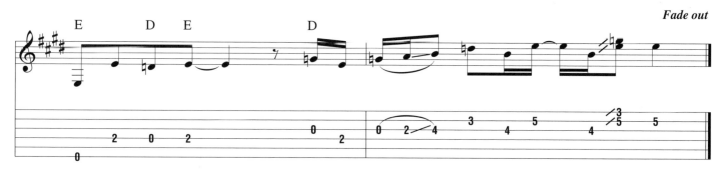

Additional Lyrics

2. If you got bad news, you wanna kick the blues, cocaine.
   When your day is done an' you wanna run, cocaine.
   She don't lie, she don't lie, she don't lie, cocaine.

3. If your thing is gone and ya wanna ride on, cocaine.
   Don't forget this fact, can't get it back, cocaine.
   She don't lie, she don't lie, she don't lie, cocaine.
   She don't lie, she don't lie, she don't lie, cocaine.

Key to the Highway

Words and Music by Big Bill Broonzy and Chas. Segar

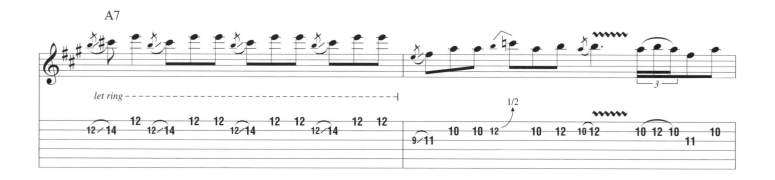

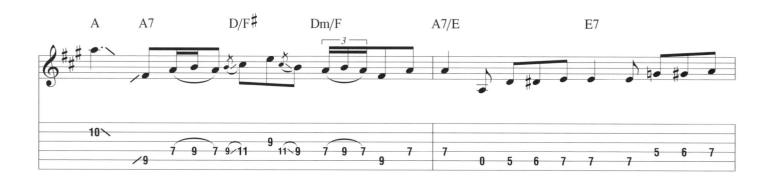

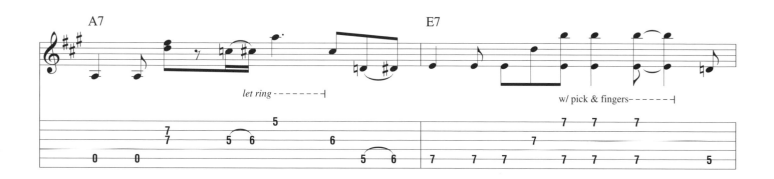

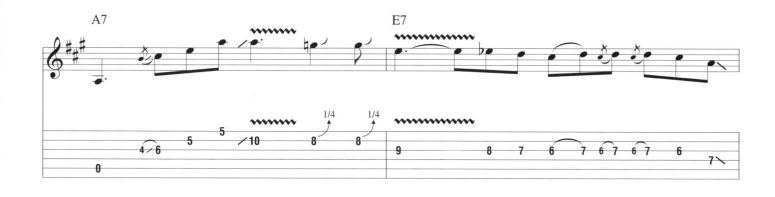

Guitar Solo

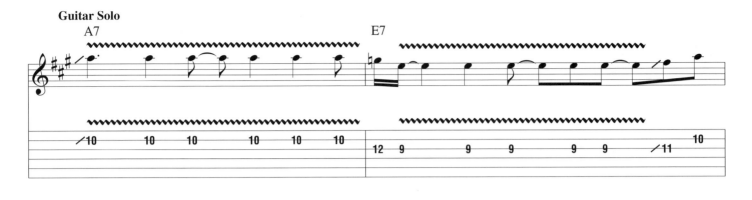

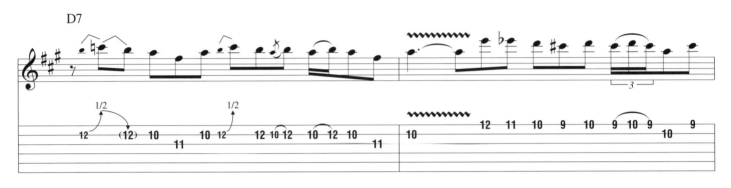

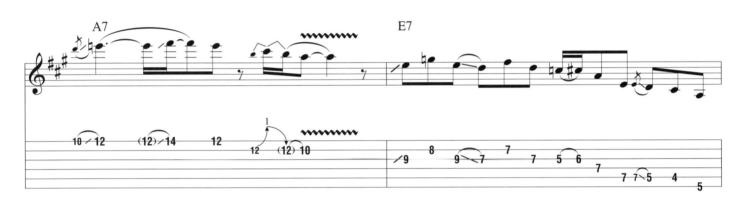

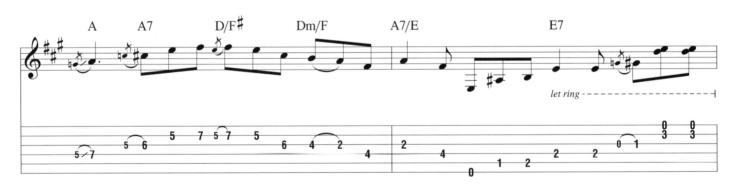

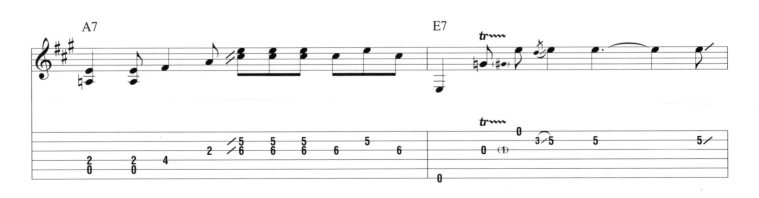

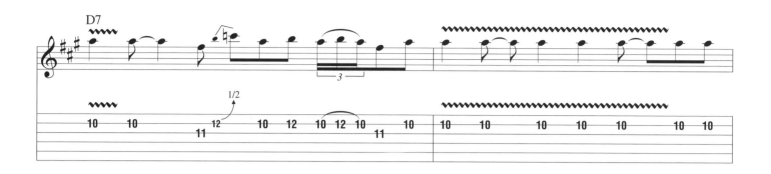

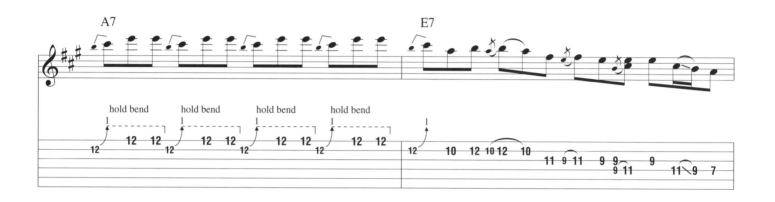

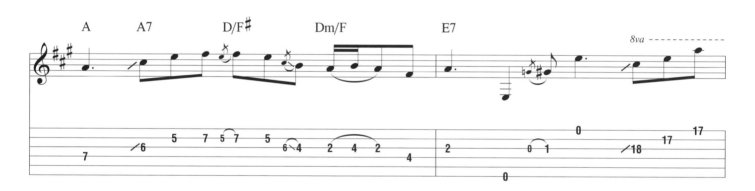

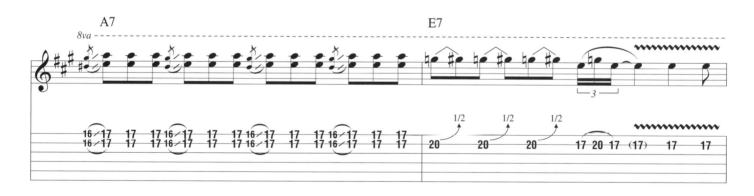

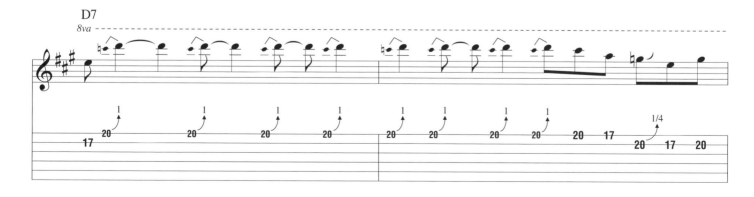

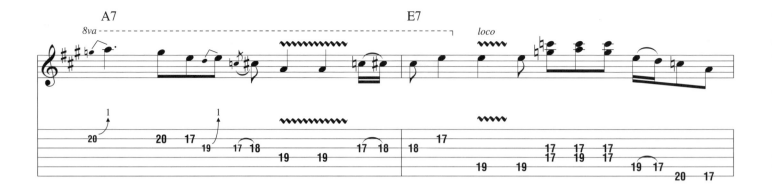

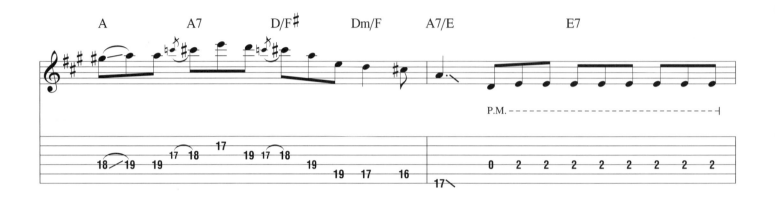

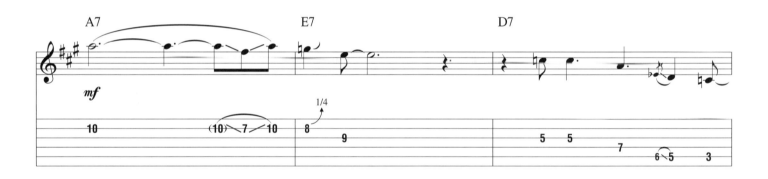

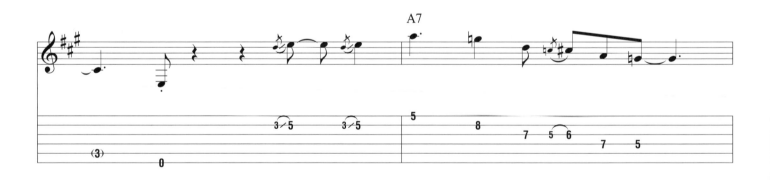

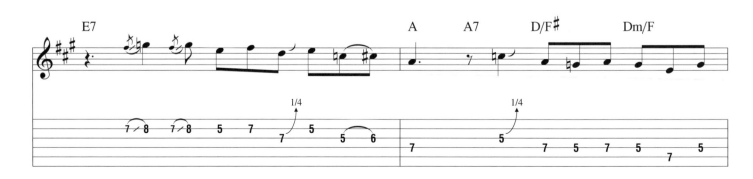

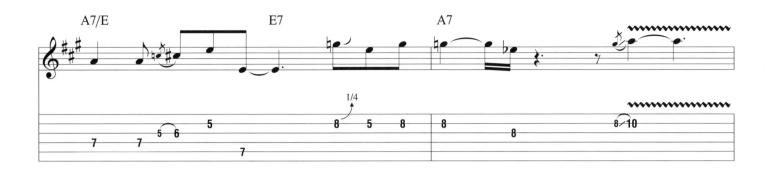

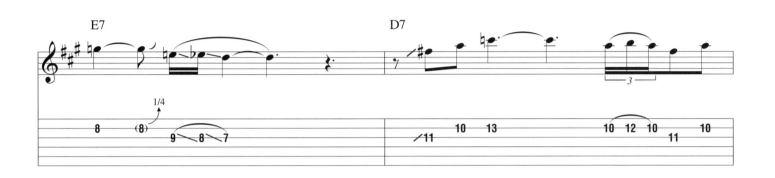

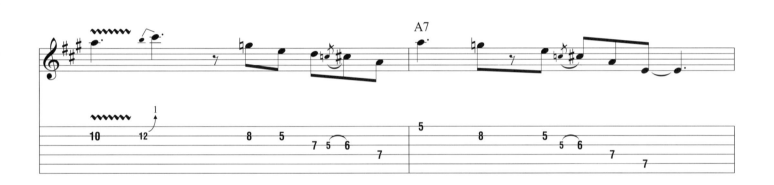

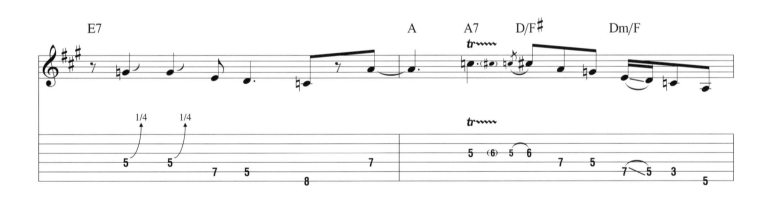

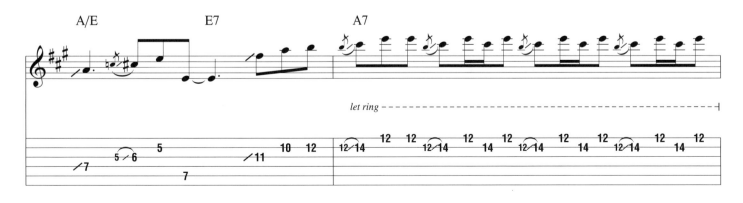

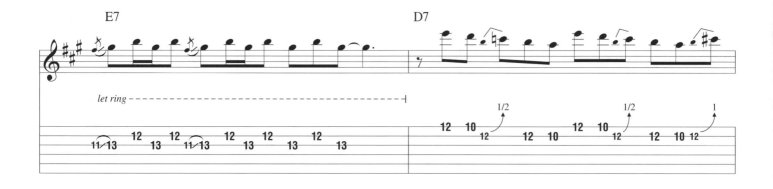

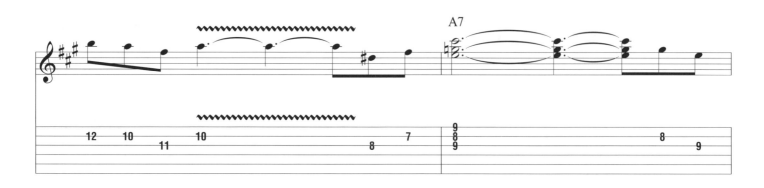

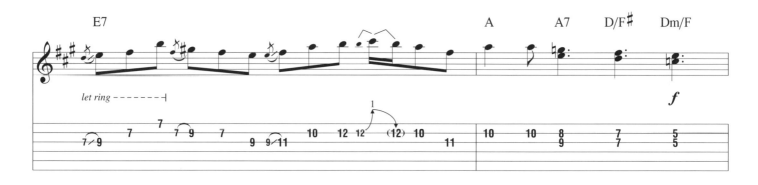

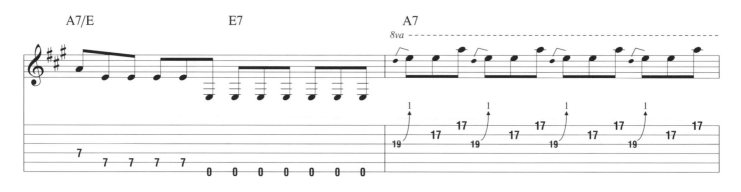

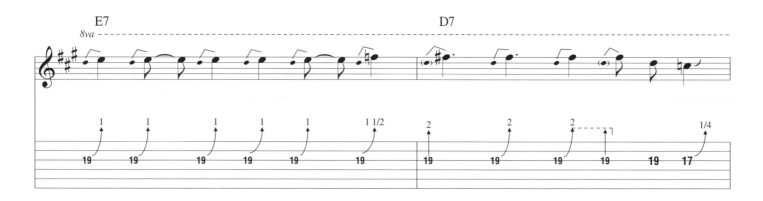

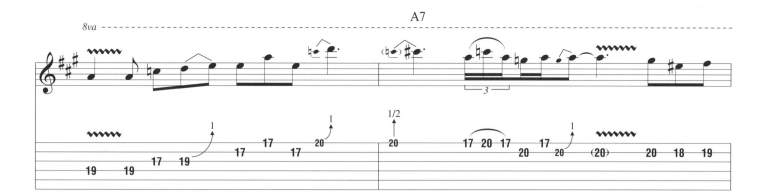

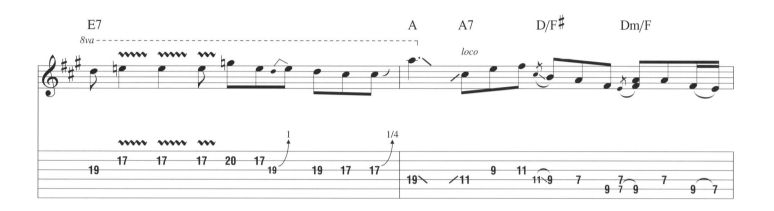

##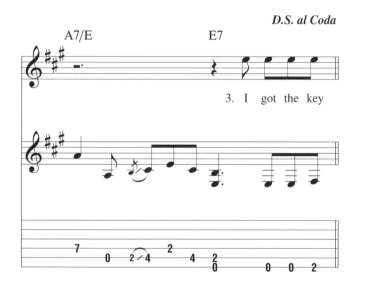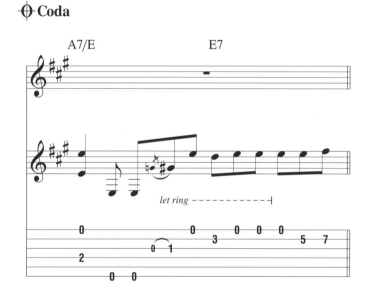

Coda

D.S. al Coda

3. I got the key

Outro-Guitar Solo

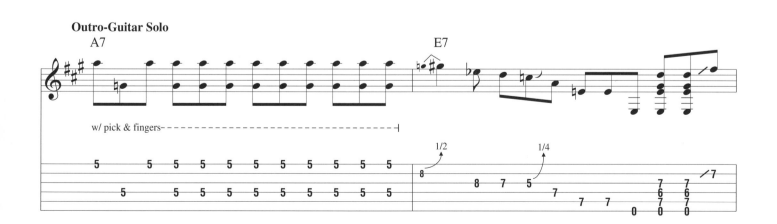

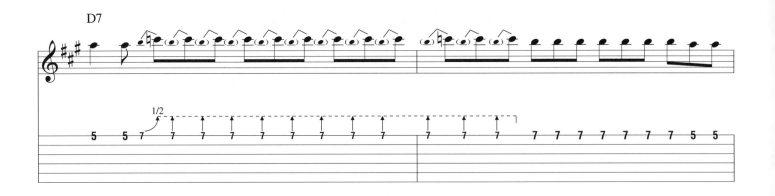

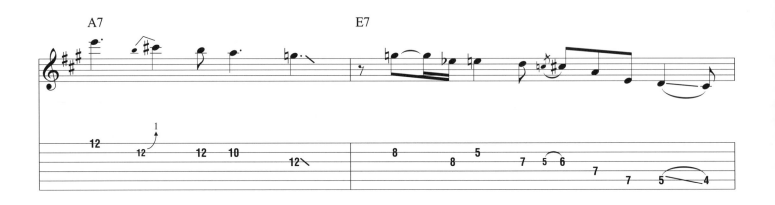

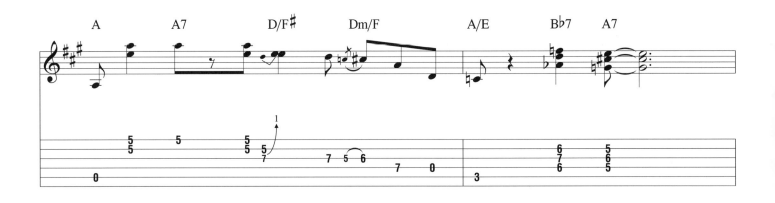

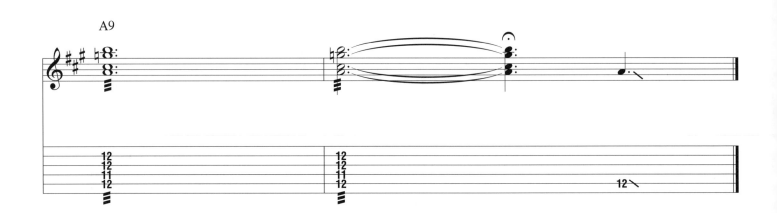

Lay Down Sally

Words and Music by Eric Clapton, Marcy Levy and George Terry

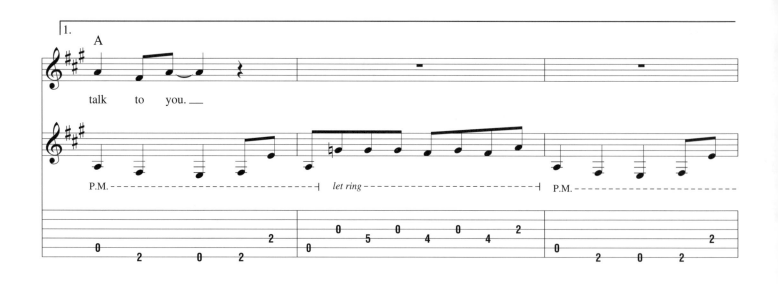

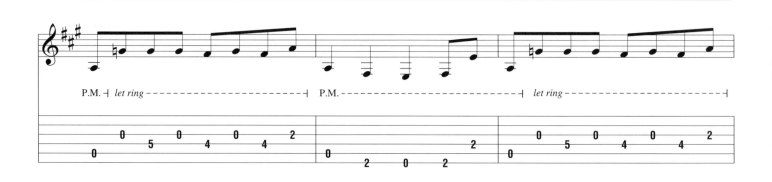

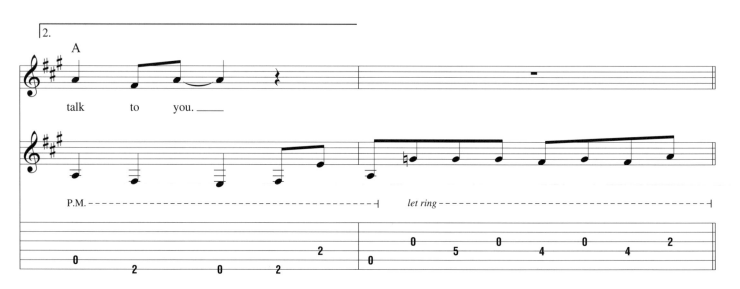

Guitar Solo

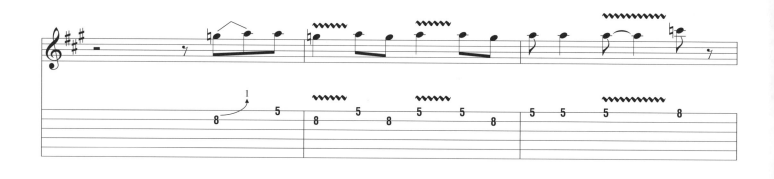

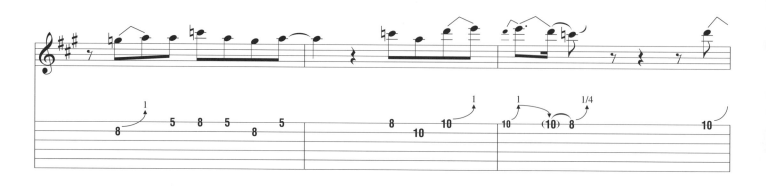

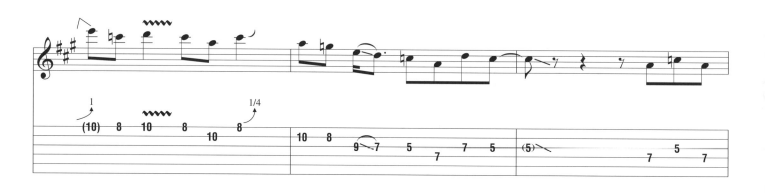

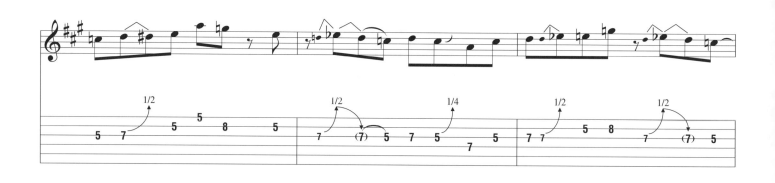

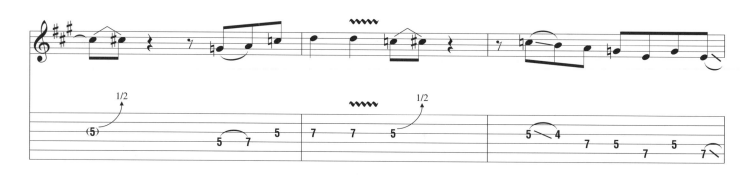

Coda 1

talk   to   you. _____

P.M.

Coda 2

talk   to   you. _____

P.M.

Outro

P.M. ———— let ring ———— P.M. ————

Additional Lyrics

2. Sun ain't nearly on the rise,
   And we still got the moon and stars above.
   Underneath the velvet skies,
   Love is all that matters. Won't you stay with me?
   And don't you ever leave.

3. I long to see the morning light
   Coloring your face so dreamily.
   So don't you go and say goodbye,
   You can lay your worries down and stay with me.
   And don't you ever leave.

White Room

Words and Music by Jack Bruce and Pete Brown

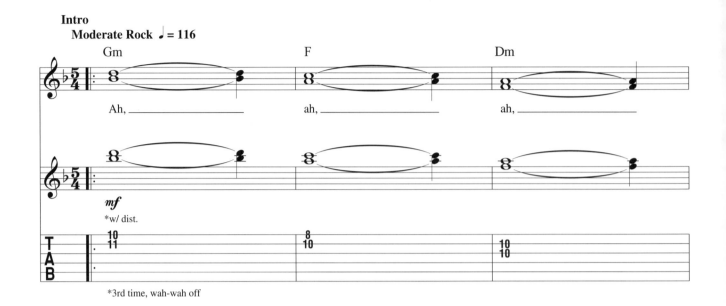

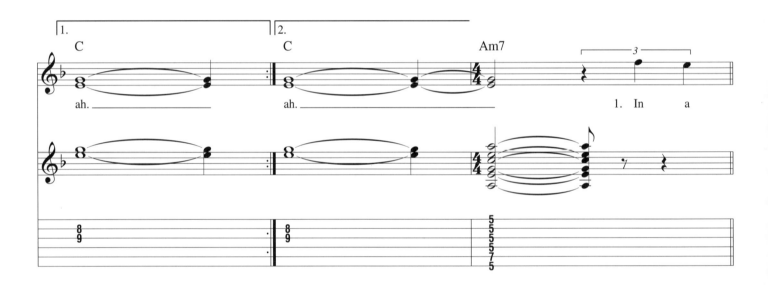

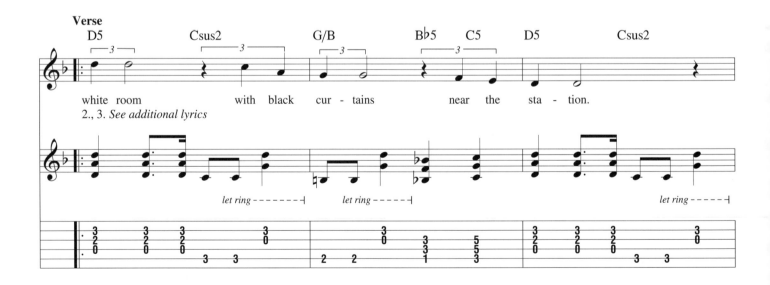

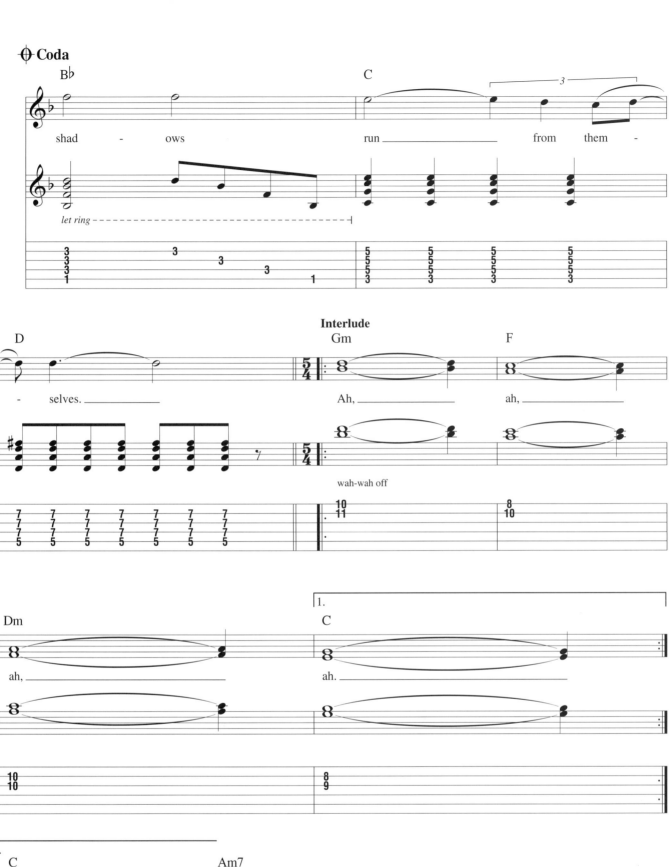

Outro-Guitar Solo

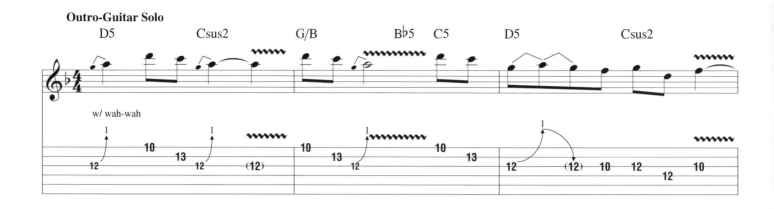

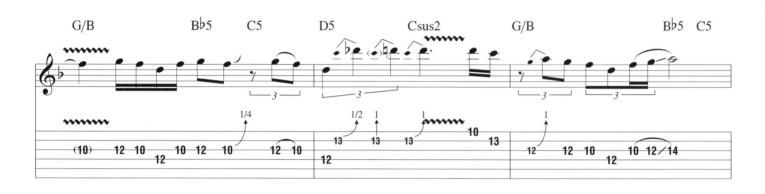

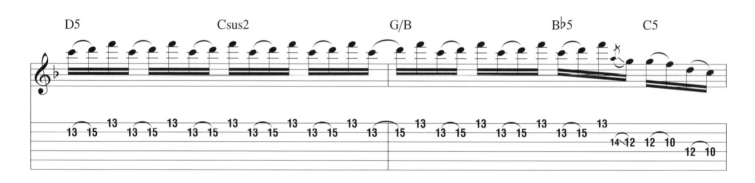

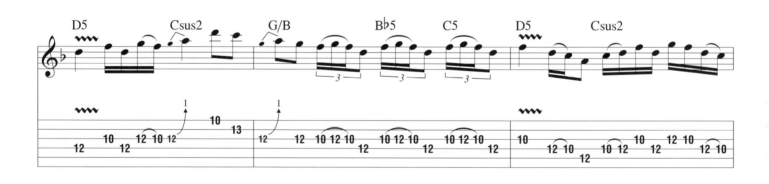

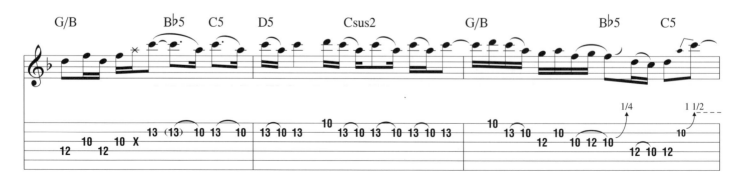

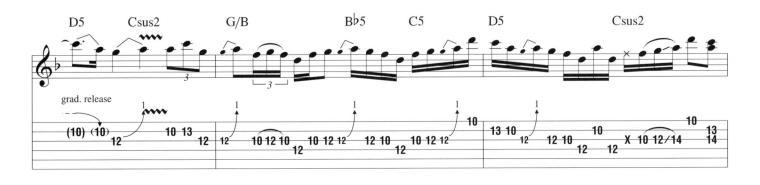

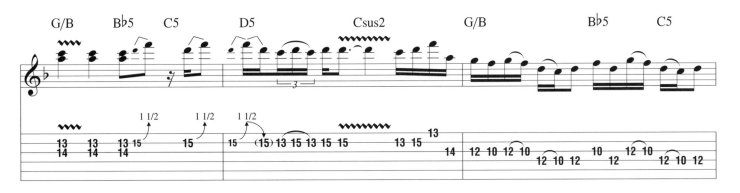

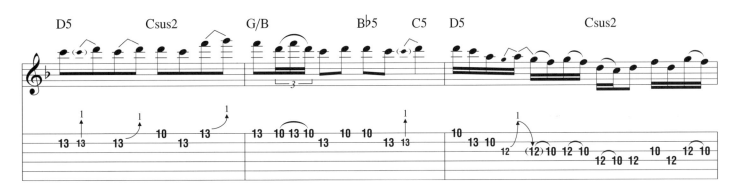

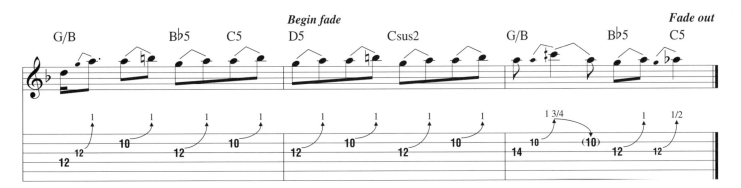

Additional Lyrics

2. You said no strings could secure you at the station.
    Platform ticket, restless diesel, goodbye windows.
    I walked into such a sad time at the station.
    As I walked out felt my own need just beginning.

Chorus 2. I'll wait in the queue when the trains come back.
    Lie with you where the shadows run from themselves.

3. At the party she was kindness in the hard crowd.
    Isolation for the old queen now forgotten.
    Yellow tigers crouched in jungles in her dark eyes.
    She's just dressing goodbye windows, tired starling.

Chorus 3. I'll sleep in this place with the lonely crowd.
    Lie in the dark, where the shadows run from themselves.

Wonderful Tonight

Words and Music by Eric Clapton

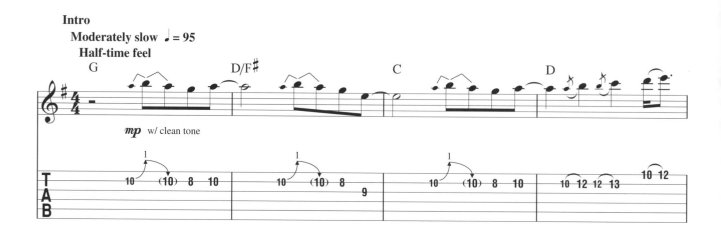

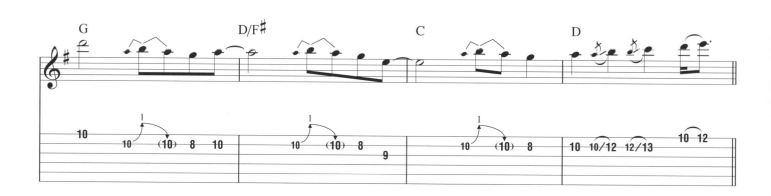

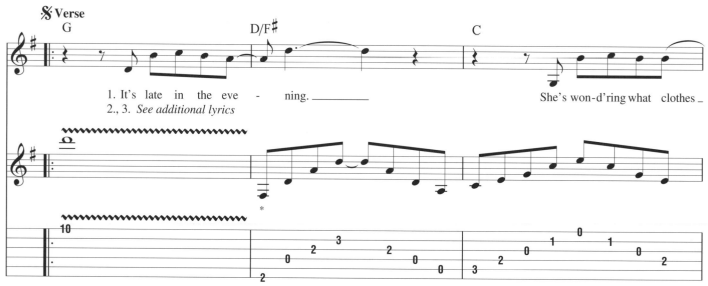

*Let arpeggiated chords ring throughout.

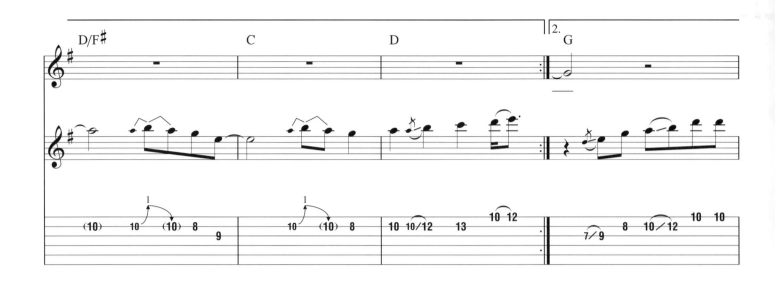

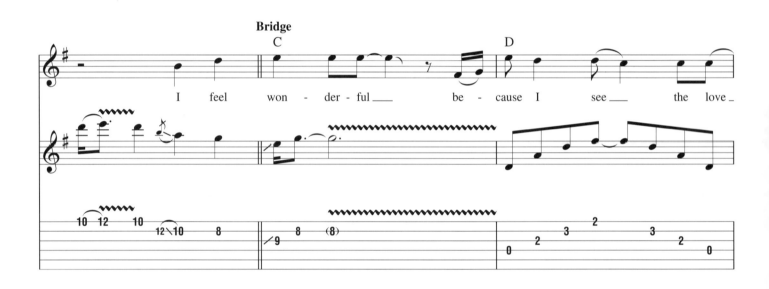

I feel won - der - ful ___ be - cause I see ___ the love ___

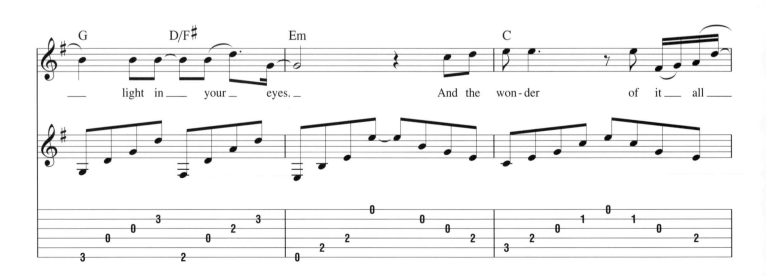

___ light in ___ your ___ eyes. ___ And the won - der of it ___ all ___

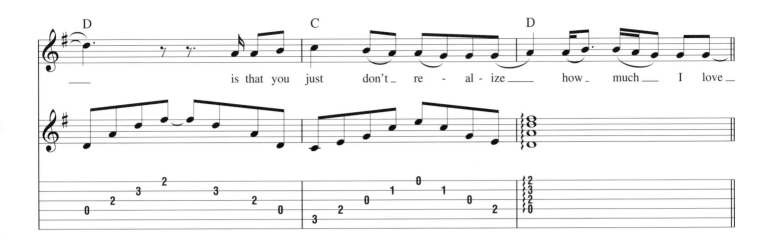

is that you just don't re-al-ize how much I love

Interlude

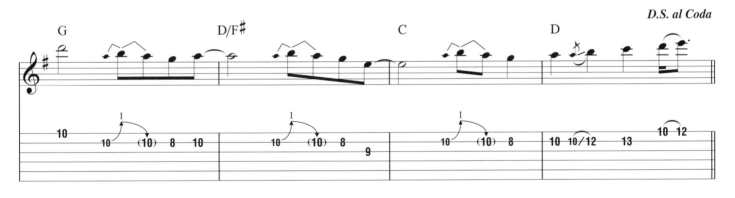

you.

D.S. al Coda

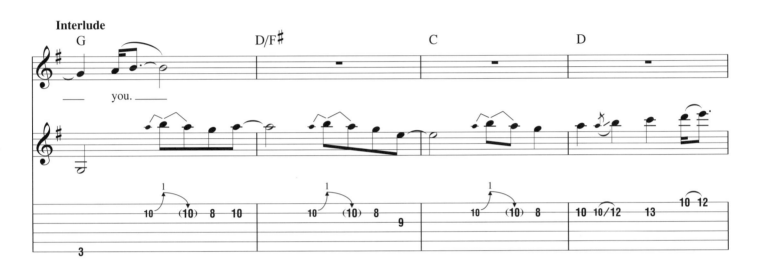

Coda

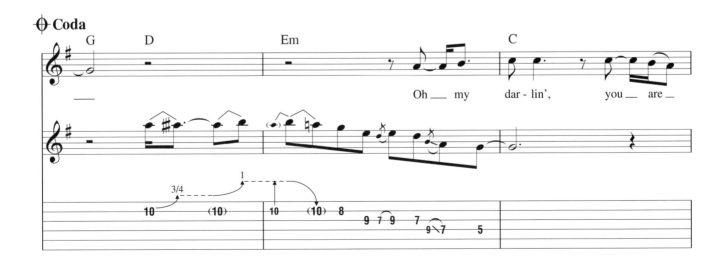

Oh my dar-lin', you are

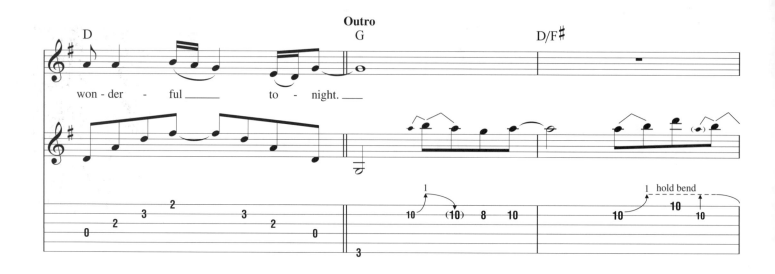

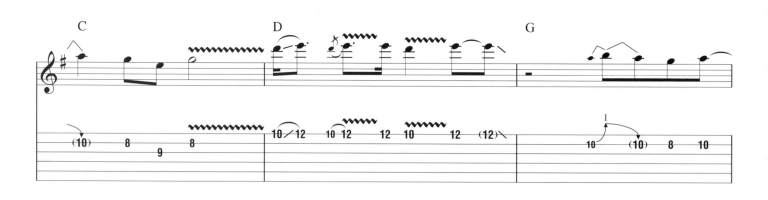

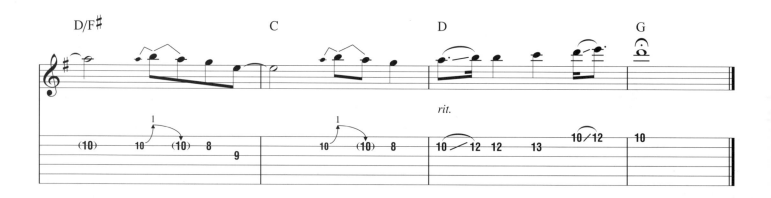

Additional Lyrics

2. We go to a party, and ev'ryone turns to see
   This beautiful lady that's walking around with me.
   And then she asks me, "Do you feel alright?"
   And I say, "Yes, I feel wonderful tonight."

3. It's time to go home now, and I've got an aching head.
   So I give her the car keys and she helps me to bed.
   And then I tell her, as I turn out the light,
   I say, "My darling, you are wonderful tonight."